To
Ian and Jean
MacInnes

The Phoenix Living Poets

FISHERMEN WITH PLOUGHS

FISHERMEN
WITH PLOUGHS
A Poem Cycle

By

George Mackay Brown

CHATTO AND WINDUS

THE HOGARTH PRESS

1979

Published by
Chatto and Windus Ltd
with The Hogarth Press Ltd
40 William IV Street
London WC2N 4DF

*

Clarke, Irwin & Co Ltd
Toronto

First published 1971
Second impression 1974
First published in paperback 1979

ISBN 0 7011 2480 6

Printed in Great Britain by
REDWOOD BURN LIMITED
Trowbridge & Esher

Some of these poems have appeared in *Scottish Poetry* (Edinburgh University Press), *Contemporary Scottish Verse* (Calder and Boyars), *An Orkney Tapestry* (Gollancz), *New Statesman, Atlantic Monthly, New Edinburgh Review, Transatlantic, English, Encounter, Scotsman, Scottish Field, Lines Review, Poetry Review, The Listener, Scottish International, Poor. Old. Tired. Horse.*

Contents

FISHERMEN WITH PLOUGHS

A Poem Cycle

A ship called *Dove* sails west out of Norway in the ninth century carrying a tribe of fisher people. Their god, the beautiful Balder, is dead. They are in flight from starvation, pestilence, turbulent neighbours (what the poet calls, in the shorthand of myth, the Dragon). But also they are compelled west by the promise of a new way of life: agriculture. The cargo in their hold is a jar of seed corn. Fate, blind and all-wise, has woven their myth about them. Now the same Fate sits at the helm.

That is the theme of the opening section of the poem.

The people settle in a valley called Rackwick in the Orkney island of Hoy. Their slow evolution through the centuries occupies the next four sections; how the climate of their existence changed with such things as the Reformation, annexation to Scotland, foreign wars, compulsory education. But essentially their lives were unchanged; the same people appear and reappear through many generations — the laird, the crofter-fisherman, the shepherd, the tinker, the beachcomber, and the women who watch the sea with stony patience; all are caught up in 'the wheel of bread' that is at once brutal and holy.

There is a slow sure improvement in the material conditions. Why does the wheel slow down and stop (V)? By the middle of this century the valley was almost completely depopulated. Perhaps (the poet argues) the quality of life grows poorer as Progress multiplies its gifts on a simple community. The dwellers in islands are drawn to the new altars. The valley is drained of its people. The Rackwick croft ruins are strewn with syrup tins, medicine bottles, bicycle frames, tattered novels, rubber boots, portraits of Queen Victoria.

In part VI the Dragon, black pentecostal fire, falls on a great city. Once again a few people escape by boat. They return to the valley. Their most precious possession is the sacred corn sack. They make themselves farmers and fishermen. The women return, unchanged yet terribly changed. But the wheel has been wrenched from the axle-tree. The great song must begin all over again, very far back, beyond the oxen and millstones and bronze throats of agriculture.

GEORGE MACKAY BROWN
September 1969

I

DRAGON and DOVE

BUILDING THE SHIP

'A dove must fold your seed from dragon flame.'
That blind rune stabbed the sea tribe.
Fishermen sought a bird in the mountains.

Their axes kept them that year from the dragon.
Logs throttled a mountain torrent.
A goatherd gaped on the lumbering tons.

Saws shrieked, sputtered, were sharpened, sang.
Dunes were pale with strewment of boards.
Seaward a keel was set.
Sprang from that spine a vibrant cluster of ribs.

Forge and anvil begot a host of rivets.
Shavings, blond hair of excited children,
Curled from the combing adzes.
A woodman died of a rotten nail.
(Njal found, near falcons, an urn for his fires.)

Men daylaboured, were dappled with lanterns.
They beat design on the thwart timbers.
Loomed a dry dove from June leafage.
That bird would unlock the horizon westwards.
Now visit, dragon, a blank shore.
Tar pots chuckled like negroes over the fires.

Moons, seven fish, swam through that labour.
A summer whirled its golden hoof.
'Trees for this doveflight,' cried Norn among the looms,
'Would blacken the coast with yawls.'
(Njal brought Gudrun down, a cold jar.)
'We sup sawdust broth,' sang the workmen.
Thorkeld drove the hammers. Their hands bled.

THE FIGHT WITH THE DRAGON

Thorkeld stood that night between Dragon and Dove.
Horn, hoofbeat, triumph of the blind mouth.
He left the hot bed of Norn his woman.
The moon was a huge cinder.
'Our guest is generous with his flames,' said Thorkeld.

Thorkeld stood in a smoulder of nets.
His cold mouth touched the sword.
'Into his fires, long sharp fish,' he said,
'See if this Dragon will relish you.'
The Dove was astir in the trestles.
At the shore the Dragon tasted the bronze fish.

Thorkeld turned. He splintered the stable door.
The mares were a row of charred skulls.
'Thunder,' he coaxed a garnet eye.
The stallion reared at the stars like a red wave.

Thorkeld unbolted the door of the women.
He plucked Gudrun from a hundred shrieks.
Hoof-fast Njal bore his manseed wombfurled waveward.

Thorkeld a blacksmith, the Dragon a blown forge.

Thorkeld stood at the altar of the god Balder.
He strewed that stone with dragon scales.
The village burned around like oil barrels.
'Now on a new shore,' said Thorkeld,
'This folk can give the star shoal a sweeter name.'
The dog Bran licked his charcoal hand.
The sun rose. Thorkeld gave himself to the sea.

Thorkeld brought to the blind westering Dove
A body charted with twelve wounds.

THE DEATH OF THORKELD

The twelve wounds were like a defiance of mouths
In a mountain ambush.
They turned, a star wheel, from the gray of dawn.
They winced like fish in a hauled net.
The twelve wounds were like a map of islands.
Women were westerlings then,
Their fingers quested among that cluster.

They are glad, all women, at a man's stillness —
In the cradle lying, quiet as apples,
In the trance after love,
Even carried in from boarfang or whalequake:
In wombfold again laid, her utter man.

Steel came unclouded from stiffening mouth.
The oarsmen could not tell tears from spindrift.
Round the last stiff smile
The shrouding women came with a drift of smiles.

An oarsman slid a silver coin for ferry
Under the cold flame of the tongue.
Skald wove deathsong in the loom of his mouth.
'Go from us, Thorkeld, among purer streams.
See, they are waiting for you,
The ancient kings asleep under the aurora.'

Norn turned down her tranquil mouth.
Throats of the heroes throbbed.

The sea opened and shut on the lord of whales.
The coat with twelve red islands
Hung, silver-clasped, from Njal's throat.

At once the blind tongue blossomed with bodings, biddings.

THE BLIND HELMSMAN OF
THE SHIP CALLED DOVE TO
THE TRIBE THAT WAS
LATELY DRAGON-EMBATTLED

Man goes, man voyages, into the blackest sun.
Nor doth hero long keep
Lithe limb or lissomness or laughter.
Honey is bitter at last in the mouth.
Fareth a shadow to the ghostly feast-halls.

And tribes decay. Northwards they seek cold fires.
Our god at last was a glacier.
Shoals departed, nets came empty to shore.
The yawl warped at the rock.
Young skippers ceased to measure the west.
Balder was ice. The mouth of the poet guttered.

But Thorkeld appraised the hooves of oxen.
Thorkeld handled the seed of the quartered sun.
Thorkeld abode a winter in Bergen
With shipwrights, westerlings, weighers of bronze.

A blind fist beat on your shutters.

It is time to turn from the solstice of black flame
And to harness the passion of oxen.
Time for the urn to be emptied.
Time for the hill to be smitten with willed fire.
Time for a hundred jars to be gathered.
Indeed it is time to forsake this ebb.
Time for the bird to seek the golden solstice.

Man goes, man voyages. Thorkeld took us
From nailing of meagre timbers.
The sailman stitched one huge gale-lover.

Man goes, man voyages. His hand swings the star wheel.
This freedom is defeat for the Dragon.

THE BLIND HELMSMAN
TO NJAL THORKELDSON
THE NEW CHIEF

I think of heroes who lived in the lissom light,
How Armod sundered the jaws of a whale,
How Kol unlocked the knees of the coldest ladies,
How Sven hooded an eagle,
How Thorkeld mingled his bronze with dragon flame.

Too soon their sun was a black circle.

This and that and the other were hewn to pieces.
One died among walrus ivories.
One silvered, hapless, into silence.

Yet none hardship like this endured.
None wounded his tribe with exile.
None ventured with poorer freight, one smouldering jar.
Seek out Gudrun, the mountain bride.
That small urn still has snow in it.
Will you brim her, like a shore girl, with oil and salt?
Gudrun must be a mother of harvesters.

Shark and sardine have swum through your tough nets.
Cod wander tinkerwise, corn is true.
Dumbness of herring, windcry and burnish of wheat.
Cornstalk unlocks the door of a great king.

Lust builds a howe over the burning ghost.
Lust, bread kissed, becomes love.

The untasted cup brimming with red circles
Will be gladness to travellers out of a storm,
To the poet after his song,
To the councillor who has spoken in the debate.
Down the dark sun
Lipflush the dove will fall with five wounds.

THE BLIND HELMSMAN
TO THE SHIPWRIGHT

In Hoy and Unst, the western landfall, shipwright,
Dry be thy beams.
Keep thy cunning from strakes awhile.
Make a door for a man and woman to stand at sunset,
A bed for mixing of hair.
Tree and tribe must mingle quiet branches.

Keep thy wit from the doomed gunwale.
Gray leafage covered those hulls.
Our fathers were shaken deathward like cold gleams.

What's Thorkeld? Torrents of silent fish.

Njal must rule from a high dovetailed bench.
Keep thy hammer from barren keels.

But the earthship, the plough, breaking frail furrows across
The slow surge of the hills,
Learn well that cleave and curve and plunge.
We are pilgrims with seed, vat-bearers.
The earthship, the coffin, under the hill drowned,
Honour that hoard of seventy years.
Njal must trade for bronze in the black grave.

Broad be your timbered barn, the great earth-ark,
To hold the cargoes of summer.
The voyagers are not lost in the loam wave.
Down the dark sun
Hurtles the dove, his beak a blazon of corn.

But still the winter images will not leave us.
We track the sun beast to his bloody lair.
At dawn our hands are red and empty.
And the Dove broods in a tangle of bitter branches.

THE NET

The first day from the weaving of the ling net
Three cod lay on the deck, gulping.
A careful gleam was put in their bellies.

The second day from the net weaving
A dogfish slapped the scuppers.
He barked at the women soundlessly.
Dog, wet or dry, is poor tooth-relish.

The third day from the net weaving
We handled a halibut on board.
The women sliced that turbulence in segments.
They wrung fierce blood in a stone jar.
(And still we tracked the gold beast into the west.)

The fourth day from the net weaving.

The fifth day from the net weaving
We gathered a mermaid into the mesh —
Njal said, a long-drowned sailor —
At least something with knuckle and rib and teeth.
Skald sullied harp with sickness.
The skull splayed streams of hair. And smiled. And sank.

The sixth day from the net weaving
A shark surged through the net.

The seventh day from the net weaving
Were bodkin, twine, snicking teeth.
The shark had laid our thousand ordered holes
In one black knot and ravel.
The second net was tougher than the first.
The eighth day from the net weaving
Herring danced in, a thousand.

GUDRUN

Gudrun's song between the salt and the corn:

'A girl is thrown on a devious wheel.
The moon took my first clay.
Coldly she turned my childhood from form to form.

The maiden jar grows tall, for ice or honey.
Swans on the lake were my sisters.
Beauty my falcon thundered from cloud to wrist.
A gelding drifted across the meadow . . .
Time eased me from the moon wheel.
Time set me on a barren stone, the solstice.

A crude workaday winter vessel,
A woman is that, said my father.
Her first honey is soon drunk.
Men use her then for oil and salt and brine.

Beauty humped like a sack in the rafters.
Njal with six young skippers
Brought me down to the jetties in the fjord.
The women stank to the elbows with glut.
Thorkeld said yes to my rages, coldness, waverings.
Thy clay is unfired, said Njal.
His throat throbbed with my small honey.

He turned on me soon with thrustings of sun seed.
Thou sweet grain jar, said Njal.

Then dragon, horseback, dove, shatters of ocean!
I cling to the wheel of the sun,
My womb throbs from curve to curve.
Far in the west, say the women,
It will come to a full fragrant barley girth.'

WHALES

Whales blundered across us, threshing lumps,
Blue hills, cartloads of thunder.
They trekked between the ice and the hidden shoals.

In the west the gold whale sank in welters of blood.
We killed that ghost each sunset.
At dawn our hands were red and empty.
Now the Dove faltered out of the blind fist.

We notched barbs on various sticks and staves.
We spread the deck with lashings of salt,
Made harpoonman of herdboy.
'Heave her to,' sang the ribbed strenuous oarsmen.
The Dove dipped into the first whalequakes.

The women wondered at all these tons of love.
Gudrun crouched in the doveflank.
Every whale was a bolted slaughterhouse,
A winter of work for candle-makers.
The priest of Balder balanced a ritual point.
That sea was huge with sacrifice.
The Dove lappered in gules of sunset.

One thunderer rose athwart the spear rank.
The barbs broke on his bulk.
Sky jaw from sea jaw split, gigantic laughter!
His frolicking rudder deluged the Dove.
His mild lip sieved the waves.
He balanced a fountain southward on his skull.

Our fires slept in the golden jar.

Far back, those floating feast-halls belched.
Soon the stars flashed around like stalks of corn.

II

OUR LADY

STATIONS OF THE CROSS

(for a chapel in the fields)

Pilate
Our winter jar of grain and malt
Is a Lenten urn.

Cross
Lord, it is time. Take our yoke
And sunwards turn.

First Fall
To drudge in furrows till you drop
Is to be born

Mother of God
Out of that mild mothering hill
And that chaste burn.

Simon
God-begun, the barley-rack
By man is borne.

Veronica
Foldings of women. Your harrow sweat
Darkens her yarn.

Second Fall
Sower-and-seed, one flesh, you stumble
On stone and thorn.

Women of Jerusalem
You are bound for the kingdom of death. The enfolded
Women mourn.

Third Fall
Scythes are sharpened to bring you down,
King Barleycorn.

Stripping
The flails creak. Golden coat
From kernel is torn.

Crucifixion
The fruitful stones thunder around,
Quern on quern.

Death
The last black hunger rages through you
With hoof and horn.

Pieta
Mother, fold him from those furrows,
Your rapt bairn.

Sepulchre
Angel, shepherd, king are kneeling, look,
In the door of the barn.

A JAR OF SALT

Twelve women stand in the darkening doors.

Our Lady of the Inshore,
Trust and *Bountiful*
Rock like kittiwakes under the crag.
Lobster and creel are separated.
The *Rose*, further out
Uncoils a long haddock line.
In the Pentland Firth
A ship, three-masted, nods
Between Norway and Ireland.
We stretch, till shroudfall,
A salt perpetual weave
Through a warp of furrows.

Our Lady of the Atlantic
Remember sailors and fishermen.

The twelve women in the crofts
Light their lamps now.
The knife is beside the stone jar.
They stand in the black thresholds.
Wind and sea meet with a new noise in the west.
They have prepared their smoke
Between sunset and the first star.

17

THE STATUE in the HILLS

Croft Women

Our Lady of Cornstalks
Our Lady of the Flail
Our Lady of Winnowing
Our Lady of Querns
Our Lady of the Oven
Blue Tabernacle
Our Lady of the Five Loaves
> Take the ploughman home
> from the ale-house sober.

Fishermen

Our Lady of the Boat
Our Lady of Oil and Salt
Our Lady of the Inshore
Our Lady of the Silver Dancers
Our Lady of Nets
Our Lady of the Atlantic
Star of the Sea
> May cuithe and codling
> hang in the chimney smoke.

Shepherds

Our Lady of Lent
Our Lady of the Last Snow
Our Lady of Muirburn
Fold of the Agnus Dei
Our Lady of Quiet Waters
Our Lady of Daffodils
Our Lady of April
> Guard the labour of
> thirty-five ewes.

Tinkers

Our Lady of Vagabonds
Our Lady of Fishbone and Crust
Our Lady of Ditch Fires

(It was a long road that,
Bethlehem to Golgotha
And you at the end Pieta, quiet chalice)
Our Lady of Pilgrims
                    We have this last can to
                    sell at the doors.

Washer Women

Our Lady of Wind and Sun
Our Lady of the Pool
(As we scrub shirts for ploughmen
Make clean our hearts, Lady)
Clother of the Child Christ
Preparer of linen for the unborn and the dead
Our Lady Immaculate
                    That these shirts be dry
                    by dewfall.

Death Watchers

Our Lady of the Last Oil
Our Lady of Silence
Our Lady of Two Candles
Mater Dolorosa
Our Lady of Dark Saturday
Stone of these stones
Our Lady of the Garden
                    Pray for old Sara cold
                    as roots.

The Croft at Night

Our Lady of Dark Ploughs
Our Lady of Furled Boats
Our Lady of Kneeling Oxen
(And their breath was warm on thy hand one
    winter)

On an old pillow, blessing
On the cradle, blessing
On those laid together in love, blessing

Our Lady of Perpetual Vigil.

19

HELMSMAN

I that was a Hoy fisherman,
A sea-troll, rifler in rock crannies
For limpet, razorfish, lobster
Have charge of a rudder
Between Spain and Byzantium.
The *Guthaland* swings in my grip.

The Bishop says, scouring salt
From paten and chalice,
'Put in under that cliff.
This voyage, pilgrims,
There's too much dice and vino.
I will say a Mass on the deck.'

And the Earl, arranging his chessmen,
'The water is sour again.
They are tired of salt beef.
Their loins are restless.
The oarsmen like olives.
They gulp that French wine like ale.
And the cabinboy with oranges
From the booths at San-Juan
Made a yellow road
All the way back to the ships.'

And Armod the Iceland poet,
'I am curious about their verse,
The formal plots,
Rose and marble and nightingale.
This is not the poetry we know,
The hawk's lonely station,
The furling, fall, unfurling,
Beauty clawed out of death.
Put me ashore at the first tavern
Among their troubadours.
I must study this rhyming.
I am anxious concerning my craft.'

Holiness, war, poetry,
One fisherman with thick shoulders.

And the oarsmen, yoked there
Like spindrift oxen,
'A queer sea, no ebb or flow.
No beer in the pubs.
Fish as small as your pinkie.
The girls dark like tinkers.
Turn the ship west, then north.
Beat the sea flat
All the way to Iceland.'

I am thinking always
'Is Gauk my mate getting lobsters
Under Rora Head?
Spring visits this coast with many roses.
Also, in May, comes our seapink.
Does Ingi, my girl, keep her body cold?'

The wind sits in the north.

And all this weighty pilgrimage,
The harp, the sword, the psalter,
I hurl at Cyprus.
The sea tears like acres of blue silk.

III

HALL and KIRK

WITCH

Three horsemen rode between the hills
And they dismounted at Greenhill.
Tall they stooped in at the door.
No long time then
Till Wilma came out among them, laughing.
The bible fishermen watched from the shore.
She sat behind the second dark rider.
They left the valley at noon.
And Wilma did not come back that day
Nor the next day
Nor any day at all that week.
And the dog barked lonely at Greenhill
And the girls took turns at milking her cow.
(One took the froth from her vat.)
The laird sent word
At the end of winter, to James of Reumin
That on Candlemas Friday
He should sail his dinghy to Kirkwall.
He sailed the *Lupin* to the red church.
And there at a steep place, Gallowsha,
Among tilted bottles, fists, faces
— A cold drunken wheel —
James saw the hangman put his red shirt on Wilma.

He sailed back smouldering
From the fire, the rum, the reproaches.
The dog of Greenhill
Barked in the throat of the valley.
And next morning
They launched their boat at the dawn with a wild shout,
The three unlucky fishermen.

A REEL of SEVEN FISHERMEN

Her hands put flame among the peats.
The old one took three fish from the smoke.
Cod off The Sneuk, drifting, an undersea song.

She sank buckets in the cold burn.
The old one broke a bannock in three.
A withershin step. A cry! A steeple of wings.

She turned quernstones, circle on circle.
The Book lay open, two white halves.
Twelve arms sought the cold dancer.

She squeezed oil in the black lamps.
The old one spread the kirkyard shirt.
Twelve feet beat on the hill, a dance.

Her hands brought fish and ale to the table.
The old one soughed, a winter thorn.
Twelve feet stood in the door, a dance.

Sea streamed like blood on the floor.
They shrieked, gull mouths.
Then bride and mother bowed to the black music.

TAXMAN

Seven scythes leaned at the wall.
Beard upon golden beard
The last barley load
Swayed through the yard.
The girls uncorked the ale.
Fiddle and feet moved together.
Then between stubble and heather
A horseman rode.

SHERIFF OF ORKNAY CONTRA IKEY FAA, EGIPTIAN OR TINKER, FOR SUNDRY BREAKINGS OF THE PEACE

Item: thou was drunk all Yule on peatbog whisky. *Item:* thou kicked the dog Patrick of Burnmouth, whereby the dog Patrick yet hirples and howls and is unable to make his customary circle about the flock. *Item:* the bone in thy dead fire was no rabbit bone but a rooster bone from the croft of Reumin. *Item:* thou encountered Anna the servant lass at The Hall, between two doors, first thy stink, then thy shadow, then thy hand, then thy mouth, then thy ragged arms, and but that Master Knarston, factor, came strictly upon thee, it had gone ill with Anna's maidenhead. *Item:* that being denied ale at Crawnest, thou wast observed to utter (as it were privily) a black word upon the oatfield there. *Item:* that thy coat is rightly the scarecrow's coat from Quoyness in Hoy.

The which villainies stand in clear proof.

Thy sentence: Piers the hangman for to follow thee thorrow the Laverock of Kirkwa and sholtie-and-cart to go on before thee and Piers for to lay about thy schamelessness the red-stripit sark.

SHROUD

Seven threads make the shroud,
The white thread,
A green corn thread,
A blue fish thread,
A red stitch, rut and rieving and wrath,
A gray thread
(All winter failing hand falleth on wheel)
The black thread,
And a thread too bright for the eye.

GRAVE STONE

Here lies Sigurd the fisherman
Dead of hooves

BUONAPARTE, THE LAIRD,
AND THE VOLUNTEERS

I, Harry Cruickshank, laird in Hoy
Being by your lordships bidden
To supply from my lands in Rackwick, Hoy,
For His Majesty's ships-of-war
Seven hale hearty willing seamen
Upon payment of the agreed bounty, two guineas,
Did thereupon name
      John Stewart at Greenhill, fisherman,
      James Stewart at Greenhill, crofter,
      William Mowat at Bunertoon, fisherman,
      Andrew Sinclair at Mucklehoose, fisherman,
      Thomas Thomson at Crowsnest, fisherman,
      James Robb at Scar, fisherman,
      James Leask at Reumin, crofter and fisherman
All unmarried, save for Wm Mowat,
Who got wife and cow from Graemsay at the fall of the year
And James Robb, a widower —
The rest all young men in their strength.
I duly rode with officers to the valley
To give notice of impressment to the said men
But found them removed
And the old people dumb and cold as stones.
One said, they were gone fishing, very far out —
Faroe, Rockall, Sulisker.
Another, to the horse-market in Caithness.
Another, "the trows were taen them aneath the hill" . . .
Upon the Sabbath following
I came to the kirk of Hoy secretely with four officers
Between the sermon and the last psalm.
We took John and James Stewart in the kirk door.
They were quiet enough after the minister spoke with them
(By this, they will be in Portsmouth.)
It is certain, my lords,
Robb and Thomson are in the caves.
Andrew Sinclair, fisherman, Mucklehoose
Listed in Hamnavoe for the Davis Straits
On the whaler *Tavistock*

31

(We found his mark and name in the agent's book)
And Mowat ferried himself to Graemsay
With wife and cow
And there hacked three fingers from his right hand
And stifled the ruin with tar.
As for Leask, he is broken with troll-music.
He lies day-long in the back of the bed,
Dark hollows about his skull.
The old woman says, "in a decline, consumption."
She stitches away at a shroud.
But like enough, the guns being silent
And Buonaparte down,
He will make his customary furrows along the hill.
A dozen old men are left in the valley.
Last week, your lordships,
I observed two women rowing to the lobsters.
Ploughmen next April will have shrill voices.

IV

FOLDINGS

THE LAIRD

Once it was spring with me
    Stone shield and sundial
Lily and lamb in the Lenten grass;
The ribs of crag and tree
    Resurrecting with birds;
In the mouths of passing crofter and fisher lass
Shy folded words.

Then one tall summer came
    Stone shield and sundial
The year of gun and rod and hawk;
The hills all purple flame;
    The burn supple with trout;
Candle-light, claret, kisses, witty talk,
Crinoline, flute.

Autumn, all russet, fell
    Stone shield and sundial
I wore the golden harvest beard.
I folded my people well
    In shield and fable.
Elders and councillors hung upon my word
At the long table.

Now winter shrinks the heart
    Stone shield and sundial
I'd quit this withered heraldry
To drive with Jock in his cart
    To the hill for peat,
Or seed a field, or from clutches of sea
Save a torn net.

CROFTER'S DEATH

They will leave this keening valley,
The daylight come.
They will dig skulls and bones
From a loaded tomb.
They will lay the hungerless back
In the old corn womb.
They will carve a name, some years
On withered stone.
The hill road will drag them back
To hunger again.
In the valley are creels for baiting,
A field to be sown.

THEN FOUR GREAT ANGELS,
   AIR, WATER, FIRE, EARTH,
   BEING SUMMONED, FELL FROM
   THEIR ETERNAL CIRCUITS UNTO
   POVERTY AT HIS SINGLE STATION,
   TO BE HIS SERVITORS

Blizzarding arcs pursue
My ploughing feet.
Through salt brimming circles
I lower my creel.
Between two querns of fire
I raise my peat.
In thundering rounds of stone
I grind my meal.

BLACK FURROW, GRAY FURROW

From the black furrow, a fecund
Whisper of dust,
From the gray furrow, a sudden
Gleam and thrust,
Crossings of net and ploughshare,
Fishbone and crust.

A WINTER BRIDE

The three fishermen said to Jess of The Shore
'A wave took Jock
Between The Kist and The Sneuk.
We couldn't get him, however we placed the boat.
With all that drag and clutch and swell
He has maybe one in a hundred chances.'
They left some mouthing cuithes in the door.
She had stood in this threshold, fire and innocence,
A winter bride.
Now she laid off her workaday shawl,
She put on the black.
(Girl and widow across a drowned wife
Laid wondering neck on neck.)
She took the soundless choir of fish
And a sharp knife
And went the hundred steps to the pool in the rock.
Give us this day our daily bread
She swilled and cut
And laid psalms and blessings on her dish.

In the bay the waves pursued their indifferent dances.

PEAT CUTTING

And we left our beds in the dark
And we drove a cart to the hill
And we buried the jar of ale in the bog
And our small blades glittered in the dayspring
And we tore dark squares, thick pages
From the Book of Fire
And we spread them wet on the heather
And horseflies, poisonous hooks,
Stuck in our arms
And we laid off our coats
And our blades sank deep into water
And the lord of the bog, the kestrel
Paced round the sun
And at noon we leaned on our tuskars
— The cold unburied jar
Touched, like a girl, a circle of burning mouths
And the boy found a wild bees' comb
And his mouth was a sudden brightness
And the kestrel fell
And a lark flashed a needle across the west
And we spread a thousand peats
Between one summer star
And the black chaos of fire at the earth's centre.

HOMAGE TO HEDDLE

'Once he disputed
The Kame with an eagle,
His two lambs
Fluttering on a sea ledge . . . .

'That storm in '75
When *Swift* and *Dolphin* vanished
He beached in Lewis
Up to the thwart in haddocks . . .

'In jail twice
For drunk fighting . . . .

'Twelve bairns called him da
In Flotta and Hoy.
Three sat at his lawful table . . . .

'And he broke six rocks
Before his plough
Stitched on the bog and heather and stone
                              of Moorfea
One green square . . . .

'He was at the whaling a winter . . . .

'An old silver man
He reads his bible now
And yawns a bit.'

NEW YEAR STORIES

We call you Hoymen up
To our Hogmanay flame
From silent kirkyards — Mans
Gone over the crag face
On a flawed rope
After some scabby sheep;
Sander whose cormorant eye a blizzard sealed
At Braga rock
The day the *Nell* was cloven;
Jock with the twenty hives,
The pale plunder of the Coolags in every hoard —
(A broken comb
Would sweeten our whisky cup);
Andrew who married eight barren wives
And buried seven
And had the cold hands of a girl to close his eye;
Jeems who fiddled drunk at every hearth
In the five islands
For wedding, funeral, birth;
Tam of the Hundred Whales.
You who by nature or bad luck are dead,
This winter night again
We summon from the earth
Before the seed.
You have unyoked out of the sun and rain,
Our brutal wheel of bread,
And are lords of legend, beyond change or chance;
We are the shadows at the brimming board.
When the lamp pales
And every story is told
And the last bottle is dry,
Be off, quickly get back
To your good silence.

IKEY CROSSES THE WARD HILL
TO THE SPANISH WRECK

Because of the Spanish wreck I tackled the hill.
I heard of the apples,
Winekegs, mermaids, green silk bale upon bale.

My belly hollowed with hunger on the hill.
From Black Meg's patch
I plucked the loan of a curl of raw kail.

We both wore patches, me and that harvest hill.
Past kirk and croft,
Past school and smithy I went, past manse and mill.

On the black height of the hill
I lay like a god.
Far below the crofters came and went, and suffered,
                                        and did my will.

I wrung a rabbit and fire from the flank of the hill.
In slow dark circles
Another robber of barrows slouched, the kestrel.

Corn and nets on the downslope of the hill.
The girl at Reumin
Called off her dog, poured me a bowl of ale.

I found no silk or brandy. A bit of a sail
Covered a shape at the rock.
Round it the women set up their terrible wail.

TWINS

Who finally never spoke in their place
On the side of the hill
— Small gestures did, nothing was left to say —
Old Howie and Merran his twin,
Questing about the hill all day like bees,
And he would go to the crags
Each morning, over the very face
For a clutch of eggs
(He liked a gull's egg fried among his bread)
And she to the burn with her pail
And maybe, on Mondays, rinse a tub of clothes;
First home would take the froth from the new ale,
Or turn in the press a wet white cheese,
But never a word said
— On such a tranquil wheel their time was spun —
Died on the same day.
They brought to the honeycomb bright brimming mouths.

FIDDLERS AT THE WEDDING

Lamps stared cold through the blond
Dishevelled day.
The bride cried out. We packed
Our fiddles away.

The bridegroom turned from the bride.
Guests by the score
Scattered with ploughs to the hill,
With creels to the shore.

IKEY'S DAY

A ditch awakening,
A bee in my hair.

Egg and honeycomb,
Cold fare.

An ox on the hill,
Gulls, ploughman, ploughshare.

A sharp wet wind
And my bum bare.

A fish-brimming corn-crammed house,
But a hard door.

Chicken, thief, and crab
Round a blink of fire.

A length of bones in the ditch,
A broken prayer.

A WARPED BOAT

As one would say, lighting an evening pipe
At a banked fire,
'Barley will soon be ripe.
Ale should be sweet in the mouth this year
With all that rain in May, though the seedtime
                                        was dry' . . . .
So Willag, before the *Merle* turned over
Rose from the rowlocks
And remarked to the open mouths on the shore,
'Drive old Bess, that fence-breaker, from the
                                        oats
Back to her patch of clover.
Yes, Breck can have my horse for his five goats.
And Jeannie is wrong again.
She raged by all that was holy I'd drown and
                                        die
In steepings of malt.
A fine evening it was for going to the sillocks.
But men,
It's a coarse drink at the end of a day, this
                                        salt.'

His sea boots filled, and Willag said no more.

A JAR OF HONEY

A woman came from every house that morning to the croft of Scar. Slowly, like holy women, they moved through the fields. Seven men stood at the end of the byre of Scar: five young men, an old man, a boy. The oat fields were yellow, gulls dipped and quarrelled over the mackerel in the bay. The men stood outside the ceremony, unwanted and useless. One of the young men shared the holy look of the women, but he too was outside their ceremony. The other men did not have a thing to say to him. They kept turning away from him. He stood there in a double isolation. A woman with huge hands and a face like stone crossed the fields, Bella of Windbreck. She walked slowly, by herself. The door of Scar opened and shut on this priestess. Now it was noon. The men at the end of the byre smoked their pipes, all but the lonely one. Once the boy chased a butterfly with a shout but the old man checked him and the boy sat down at a fissure in the wall, watching bees oozing out and in. A girl, an acolyte, crossed over to the burn from Scar for water. With a pure white look on her she passed the men and returned, silent and intent, a heavy brimming pail at each side of her. Another woman came out for peats, her arms red from the flame. The sun dragged through the afternoon like an ox through furrows. Suddenly the water girl stood in the open door of Scar, her arms wild circles. 'Simon!' she cried. 'Come now.' The young man turned his burnished face to the house. He wouldn't move. He was afraid of the elemental women inside there, with their water and fire, the terrible priestess and her servers, swaddlers, shrouders, guardians of the gate of birth and the gate of death. He couldn't move. The other young men were laughing all round him now. They laid earth-coloured hands on him. They buffeted him gently. They turned his face towards the open door. Two of them walked with him, one at each side, to the threshold. He went inside alone. The boy sat at the end of the wall, gray wax at his mouth, his fingers threaded with honey. The old man knocked out his pipe, spat, lifted six creels from the wall, and slowly walked down to the boats.

48

A young man lifted a scythe from the end of the barn. He
began to whet it on a red stone.
The gate of life had been opened.
Between that and the dark gate were the fish and the
fleece and the loaf, the oil jars and the jars of salt and
the jars of grain, and the one small jar of honey.

FOLDINGS

What they fold, what the shepherds fold,
Is this, in March
A mothering huddle.

The crofter's trade a hoarding, folding,
                                    burnishing
Of seed from snow.

What the fishermen fold is this,
A sklinter of haddocks
From the breached Atlantic banks.

What the women fold
Are torn nets, a stretch of yarn from
                            the loom,
Sheaf after sheaf of August oats,
In the cupboard cheese and honey and ale
                            and bread,
Shapes in the womb,
Night long as a shroud when the twelve
                            boats
Are drifting lights in the west
And the ebb ravels itself in rock and
                            sand.

A winter bride is ravished with plough
                            and seed
And finds at last
The crag where mother and widow enfolded
                            stand.

JOCK

Winter

The valley changed its patches
For one seamless coat.
Jock trudged out to find
His nine snowtranced sheep and Madrum
           his goat.

He dug them from bright graves
Among the Coolag hills,
All but one ewe whose bones
Are lost again in a drift of daffodils.

Spring

First, to get to his plough,
Jock thrust aside
A lantern, a litter-and-bitch,
Twelve lobster boxes, a fiddle bow,
A gun, and a coffin half-made.
(He had spent a winter night in the ditch.
It was after the feast of the saint of
           ploughmen, Burns.
He was shuttled through with a pure warp of
           barley.
That way, he nearly died.)
He turned some sacks and found the rusted blade.
He stirred that powerful curve from its
           winter trance.
'So there you are, Mister Plough.
It's you and me and the mare for the hill
           early.
You tried to kill me, I know,
In January, you and your golden bairns.
But that's all past. I'm giving you one
           more chance.'

Summer

Who thronged the dinghy with bronze and silver
           each sunset? Jock.
Who took the coats from the sheep? Jock.

Who put Bella's Sunday hat on the scarecrow? Jock.
Who got drunk at the seven agricultural shows? Jock.
Who carted home winter fire? Jock.
Who led the bull round the twelve crofts? Jock.
(Also Jock, the day the minister called,
Was locked in the byre.)

Autumn

The corn breaks, wave after wave,
On Kringnafea.
Crofts lie strewn, transfigured wrecks
In a fenceless sea.

Larks in the golden spindrift
And bees, are drowned.
Then Jock, a Canute with a scythe,
Turns the wave round.

They salvage the cargoes of summer,
The barley, the oats.
Tall women stoop among the sheaves
With bronze throats.

FUNERAL

Came, their eyes four puddles, the women
of Park.
Came, with a flagon of whisky, Quernstones.
(And the biggest bowl was filled
And a honeycomb broken
And a pot of water hung over the
red-tongued peat.)
Came the nose of the cat and quizzed the
tied jaw,
Cold kissing cold.
Came the minister, a black column of words.
Came the five bairns of Bunertoon, hill
dancers,
But furled their feet in the door.
Came an old one with a shroud
(And drenched the house with grief,
biography, mothballs).
Came the fisherman's wife with a dish of
salt
And a jar of oil.
Came the wife of Greups with circles of
smoking bread.
The widow sat in his chair, a black queen.

PLOUGHMAN and WHALES

The ox went forward, a black block, eyes
                              bulging,
The mouth a furnace.
Tammag went forward, cursing.
The plough wavered between them.
And gulls plagued Tammag, a whirl of
                              savage snow
On the field of the sun.
Twice the plough struck stone,
A clang like a bell
Between the burning hills and the cold sea.
Tammag clawed his shoulder. He cursed.
And the ox belched lessening flame.
Six furrows now and a bit . . . .
Suddenly Tammag heard it, low thunder
Far in the firth,
And saw blue surging hills, the whales
On trek from ocean to ocean.
They plunged, they dipped, they wallowed,
They sieved a million small fish through
                              their teeth.
The sun stood at the hill, a black circle.
The shore erupted with men and boats,
A skirl of women,
Loud dogs, seaward asylums of gulls.
The ox stood in the seventh furrow
In a dream of grass and water.
'Tammag!' the boatmen cried. 'Tammag!'
Tammag wiped his silver face on his sleeve.
He yelled at the ox. The plough wavered.
                              They stumbled on.
They tore from the black sun
Loaf, honey-comb, fleece, ale-jar, fiddle.

V

THE STONE HAWK

LOVE LETTER

To Mistress Madeline Richan, widow
At Quoy, parish of Voes, in the time of hay:

The old woman sat in her chair, mouth
agape
At the end of April.
There were buttercups in a jar in
the window.

The floor is not a blue mirror now
And the table has flies and bits of
crust on it.

Also the lamp glass is broken.

I have the shop at the end of the
house
With sugar, tea, tobacco, paraffin
And, for whisperers, a cup of whisky.

There is a cow, a lady of butter, in
the long silk grass
And seven sheep on Moorfea.

The croft girls are too young.
Nothing but giggles, lipstick, and
gramophone records.

Walk over the hill Friday evening.
Enter without knocking
If you see one red rose in the window.

HADDOCK FISHERMEN

Midnight. The wind yawing nor-east.
A low blunt moon.
Unquiet beside quiet wives we rest.

A spit of rain and a gull
In the open door.
The lit fire. A quick mouthful of ale.

We push the *Merle* at a sea of cold flame.
The oars drip honey.
Hook by hook uncoils under The Kame.

Our line breaks the trek of sudden thousands.
Twelve nobbled jaws,
Gray cowls, gape in our hands,

Twelve cold mouths scream without sound.
The sea is empty again.
Like tinkers the bright ones endlessly shift
                              their ground.

We probe emptiness all the afternoon;
Unyoke; and taste
The true earth-food, beef and a barley
                              scone.

Sunset drives a butcher blade
In the day's throat.
We turn through an ebb salt and sticky
                              as blood.

More stars than fish. Women, cats, a gull
Mewl at the rock.
The valley divides the meagre miracle.

THE LAIRD'S FALCON

The falcon on the weathered shield
   Broke from his heraldic hover
   To drift like a still question over
The fecund quarterings of the field.

Doves in that dappled countryside,
   Monotones of round gray notes,
   Took his bone circle in their throats,
Shed a mild silence, bled, and died.

All autumn, powered with vagrant blood
   (But shackled to a silken call)
   He paced above the purple hill,
His small black shadow tranced the wood.

Steadfast himself, a lord of space,
   He saw the red hulk of the sun
   Strand in the west, and white stars run
Their ordered cold chaotic race;

Till from lucidities of ice
   He settled on a storied fist,
   A stone enchantment, and was lost
In a dark hood and a sweet voice.

SEA RUNES

Five Crags
The five black angels of Hoy
That fishermen avoid —
The Sneuk, The Too, The Kame, Rora, The Berry.

Elder
Charlag who has read the prophets
A score of times
Has thumbed the salt book also, wave after wave.

Crofter-Fisherman
Sea-plough, fish-plough, provider
Make orderly furrows.
The herring will jostle like August corn.

Shopkeeper
Twine, sea stockings, still to pay
And Howie trading
Cod for rum in the ale-house.

New Boat
We call this boat *Pigeon*.
Go gentle, dove
Among skuas, easterlies, reefs, whalebacks.

Fishmonger
The fishmonger stood at the rock
With bits of dull silver
To trade for torrents of uncaught silver.

THE SCARECROW IN THE
SCHOOLMASTER'S OATS

Hail, Mister Snowman. Farewell,
Gray consumptive.

Rain. A sleeve dripping.
Broken mirrors all about me.

A thrush laid eggs in my pocket.
My April coat was one long rapture.

I push back green spume, yellow breakers.
King Canute.

One morning I handled infinite gold,
King Midas.

I do not trust Ikey the tinker.
He has a worse coat.

A Hogmanay sun the colour of whisky
Seeps through my rags.
I am — what you guess — King Barleycorn.

A CHILD'S CALENDAR

No visitors in January.
A snowman smokes a cold pipe in the yard.

They stand about like ancient women,
The February hills.
They have seen many a coming and going, the hills.

In March, Moorfea is littered
With knock-kneed lambs.

Daffodils at the door in April,
Three shawled Marys.
A lark splurges in galilees of sky.

And in May
A russet stallion shoulders the hill apart.
The mares tremble.

The June bee
Bumps in the pane with a heavy bag of plunder.

Strangers swarm in July
With cameras, binoculars, bird books.

He thumped the crag in August,
A blind blue whale.

September crofts get wrecked in blond surges.
They struggle, the harvesters.
They drag loaf and ale-kirn into winter.

In October the fishmonger
Argues, pleads, threatens at the shore.

Nothing in November
But tinkers at the door, keening, with cans.

Some December midnight
Christ, lord, lie warm in our byre.
Here are stars, an ox, poverty enough.

BEACHCOMBER

Monday I found a boot —
Rust and salt leather.
I gave it back to the sea, to dance in.

Tuesday a spar of timber worth thirty bob.
Next winter
It will be a chair, a coffin, a bed.

Wednesday a half can of Swedish spirits.
I tilted my head.
The shore was cold with mermaids and angels.

Thursday I got nothing, seaweed,
A whale bone,
Wet feet and a loud cough.

Friday I held a seaman's skull,
Sand spilling from it
The way time is told on kirkyard stones.

Saturday a barrel of sodden oranges.
A Spanish ship
Was wrecked last month at The Kame.

Sunday, for fear of the elders,
I sit on my bum.
What's heaven? A sea chest with a thousand
                                    gold coins.

WINDFALL

No red orchards here; the sea
    Throbbing, cold root
To salt incessant blossoming
    Burdens the net
    With gray and with white and with blue fruit.

GIRL

In that small school
Learn number and word
And the ordered names.
    Then older knowledge, a kinder spell:
To lift your latch
To neighbour and tramp
Till all share
Fish, bread, and ale
At your brimming board.
    Elders and minister, what do they say?
Among the flames
Of April lust
Be cold as snow —
Let fishermen come and crofter go.
    Learn this last wisdom:
Beyond gray hair,
A winter lamp,
A leaking thatch,
You must enter the halls of the kingdom,
Persephone,
Of passionate dust.

OLD MAN

'Before the cuckoo puts his two notes
                              over the burn —
The wings crowd south
Flight by fall
The birds return

'What with rheumatics, asthma, and
                              whisky the price it is —
The sap sinks
Shower by spring
The waters rise

'Peerie Tam will have my plough, and
                              my fiddle, and oars.'
Come, dancer, go
Step by circle
The reel endures.

ROADS

The road to the burn
Is pails, gossip, gray linen.

The road to the shore
Is salt and tar.

We call the track to the peats
The kestrel road.

The road to the kirk
Is a road of silences.

Ploughmen's feet
Have beaten a road to the lamp and barrel.

And the road from the shop
Is loaves, sugar, paraffin, newspapers, gossip.

Tinkers and shepherds
Have the whole round hill for a road.

BUTTER

What's come of my churning? The van-man,
he took seven pounds, and a basket of warm
eggs, for jam, sugar, tea, paraffin. I gave the
tinkers a lump, to keep the black word from
our byre. I put some on the damp peats, to
coax a flame. I swear the cat has a yellow
tongue. There was only a scrape for the
fisherman's bannock, like a bit of sun on a
dull day. The old cow is giving me a mad
look.

THE COWARD

All Monday he sat by the fire, Stoney
           the fisherman
Loud with the hoast,
Till Jean bought a certain nostrum from
           the van.
In terror at the black stuff in the bottle,
When Jean was out, luring eggs from the
           hen,
He coughed his way to the noust
And launched the *Belle* with a roll and
           a rattle
Into a sea
Shaken with spasms as loud and green
           as he.
He came back late
With a score of lobsters, sillocks like
           stars, a skate
As wide and bright as the moon
And devil a hoast.
He felt as rich as the laird as he landed his creels.
But there, a patient Penelope on the coast,
Stood Jean with a spoon
And the phial that, warts to consumption,
           cured all ills.

SABBATH

On the first morning I lisped your name.
The school bell rang.
We stood at the blackboard, two unlettered pigeons.

The second morning
You set a scarecrow between plough and quern.
You wove a creel.
In my mother's croft I learned to smoke fish, the song
of the wheel, brewing.

I went down to the shore to meet five boats from nine
In a lull of the storm.
You came out of the smother, a ghost with a red mouth.
That was the third morning.

The fourth morning the women put white things on me.

Between fifth morning and sixth morning, darkness,
A dozen moons that gathered to gouts of blood.
I worked the croft alone.
That was the year of the submarine.
Men sank and burned.
Women turned slowly to stone.
The sixth lamplight a stranger stood in the door,
A man from the west.
I knew that red mouth through the surge of beard.
It blew the lamp out.
Our lost sun pulsed between us.
Were rootings of good seed on a gaunt acre.

Now in the Sabbath
We mix complaint and blessing, two scripture doves.

HILL RUNES

Thirst
Horse at trough, thrush in quernstone,
The five ploughmen
Much taken up with pewter.

Elder
Andrew who has read the gospel
Two or three times
Has quizzed the clay book also, furrow by furrow.

Smithy
The flames of love, the hammerings, glowings,
End one way —
A cold nail on an anvil.

Kirkyard
Between stone poem and skull
April
Touches rat, spade, daffodil.

Tractor
The horsemen are red in the stable
With whisky and wrath.
The petrol-drinker is in the hills.

THE BIG WIND

The big wind trundled our pail, a
                    clanging bell
Through the four crofts,
Broke the clean circles of wave and
                    gull,
Laid the high hay in drifts,
Beat down the stones of the dead,
Drove the *Beagle* aground,
Whirled up Merran's petticoats round
                    her head,
And set three hen-houses (cockerels raging aloft)
                    on the crested Sound.

The kestrel stood unmoving over the hill.

THE DROWNING BROTHERS

The boy said (his arm a long white stone)
'The burn is a fish in a net of fences . . . .
The burn is a glancing shuttle . . . .'
A crofter turned a homing rudder.
Corn, a prodigal, stood in the door of the sun
Arrayed in harvest patches.
The crofter beached. The ripe hands of the wind
Throttled his haddocks.
He shouted the women from loom and fire.

The brother said (his thigh a struck gleam)
'The burn is a lark in a cage. The silver tongue
Yearns on and out . . . .'
The burn throbbed between hills and beach all day.
Pigeons fretted the stubble.
Women stooped to the sheaves with bronze throats.

The first boy said (half marble and half flesh)
'The tinker burn hurries from field to field.
He begs for small things.
Heather to cornstalk to seaweed he burbles gossip.
He spreads his pack at every stone,
Torrents of sapphire and lace,
Among the reeds a swatch of green silk . . . .'
An oat, a can, a straw, left the slow valley.
Ikey slouched at the stubble edge,
Banished that day with larks, rats, fishermen.

The brother said (his throat a sculpted psalm)
'The burn is our angel. He praises.
He fills our pails.
He flames in the face of the drinking beasts.
He carries the valley filth
Out to the seven brightnesses of the bay.
He has turned a key.
Quick, now, follow the cold one.
They will drag us back to their old sweat and dung . . . .'
Those hills, The Ward and Moorfea, brooded upon them,
Dark angels.

The tractor throbbed with one urgent image, bread.

Heavy with images, the statues drowned.

FISHERMAN'S BRIDE

Around us a muted din
   Of fiddles and feet,
      Circlings of bread and ale.
This room we are in
   At the seaward side, is still.
      I turn a cold sheet.

Midnight. The shoal drifts
   Like a host of souls unborn, along the shore.
      The tide sets from the west.
His salt hand shifts
   From tumults of thigh and breast
      To the hard curve of an oar.

DEAD FIRES

At Burnmouth the door hangs from a broken hinge
And the fire is out.

The windows of Shore empty sockets
And the hearth coldness.

At Bunertoon the small drains are choked.
Thrushes sing in the chimney.

Stars shine through the roofbeams of Scar.
No flame is needed
To warm ghost and nettle and rat.

Greenhill is sunk in a new bog.
No kneeling woman
Blows red wind through squares of ancient turf.

The Moss is a tumble of stones.
That one black stone
Is the stone where the hearth fire was rooted.

In Crawnest the sunken hearth
Was an altar for priests of legend,
Old seamen from the clippers with silken beards.

The three-toed pot at the wall of Park
Is lost to woman's cunning.
A slow fire of rust eats the cold iron.

The sheep drift through Reumin all winter.
Sheep and snow
Blanch fleetingly the black stone.

From that sacred stone the children of the valley
Drifted lovewards
And out of labour to the lettered kirkyard stone.

The fire beat like a heart in each house
From the first cornerstone
Till they led through a sagging lintel the last old one.

The poor and the good fires are all quenched.
Now, cold angel, keep the valley
From the bedlam and cinders of A Black Pentecost.

VI

THE RETURN
OF THE WOMEN

LANDFALL

Jane

They put on pasteboard helmets and greaves. The Trojans
retired behind a high battlement (a pile of desks and the
blackboard.) The Greeks stood, a clamant wedge, in the
middle of the room. Class IVC would soon mell in the
breached wall. Helen with her blunt freckled nose sat
in the window-seat; she looked down from a high turret.
An ox-eyed Juno, I directed their comings and goings.
Ulysses took off his glasses and breathed on the left lens.
Achilles stood beside the globe of the world. *And before
this day's battle is done,* he piped, *full many a soul will
be ferried across the Styx.* Hector astride a desk brand-
ished his ruler, he shouted defiance. It was our con-
tribution to the school concert, the second day of
rehearsal. Far too soon, Troy began to burn. The class-
room dappled and darkened. Fire bowed through the
door, a mad inspector. His red tongue flickered in my
face. Then he turned to interrogate the players —
forty boys and girls smouldered around him like rag
dolls. The play was over. Through curtains of ash I
came at last to the smell of the sea. Was it night? Cold
wet masses moved against a sagging wharf. I went from
one burnt element into another, till I must have been
only a spread of hair on the burnt sea. Then hands
upgathered me from the suck and drench. Oars creaked.
Voices besieged my face but no mouths moved.
Of course she's blind, said a voice. *She won't do. Let
her go.* I touched the beard that kind golden words
were coming out of. I said in a changed voice (for
this was the meeting place of the dead beside the
waters, with antique masks) *I pray you, good ferryman,
have a pity of me, let me sink. I would not look again on
the shadows of labour and love.* Goldenbeard held me
closer to him. *Poor lass,* he said, *God help you, you
won't do that. Your eyes are cinders.* His body strained
and swayed above me. He smote, with other oarsmen,

81

sounding furrows. He said, after a time, *They can generally see more than other folk, the blind.*

Natasha

The boat is wrapped round and about in swathes and cerements of fog. The people in the stern move like ghosts. But the petrel assures me that we aren't a cargo of dead people — it spurts out of the fog, it dips and hovers, it puts a sweet askance look over the *Truelove* and her voyagers. At least, though my violin is lost in The Black Flame — and all books and statues too, I think — we won't have to live in a birdless world. Yesterday I saw a seal or a porpoise, very indistinct, on the surface (or it could have been a bottle with the world's last message in it). The petrel again — it insists *This way! This way!* The men tug hard at the oars in rising sea, spindrift salts in, sifts in, Saul the Skipper throws an oilskin over the sack of seed corn. A chasm of purple sky — one cerement is lifted from our sea shroud, then dropped again, but a few stars pulsed like boys bathing (choristers in a rockpool). The petrel again — I love these birds, the lost cold drifting sea syllables.

Bianca

Night. Then morning again, and sea and sky one huge opaque pearl. The same day after day. This afternoon the fog lifted — we were among black islands — bone and rottenness everywhere, even on these western beaches. (Nothing for me to do but sometimes bathe the eyes of the blind schoolteacher and swab an occasional vomit from the deck. I studied vigilance and patience a long time ago.) In a few days these educated people have broken back into the narrow circle of the beasts. The antics of life are performed openly. They eat and relieve themselves and — a few of them — make love like floating dogs. Sunset. They'll soon be at it again. I was changing bandages in St Lawrence's — an old man who had spilled a kettle over himself — when The Black Flame burst the hospital open. It cancelled all salves and bandages, the city was one complete scald. I will have to be very patient, make myself a stone in the middle of these fires. Some day they may need me. I don't know. That's Venus, and I think up there, now, very faintly, The Plough.

Sophie

David chose me in the river estuary. We hadn't been in the boat a half-hour. First thing he did was beg this bit of canvas from The Skipper — it covers a part of us at least after dark. *That wedge of thick blackness to starboard last night*, he says, *that was Glasgow* . . . *And here*, he says, *is Jura with the three breasts*. (He used to climb and sail a lot in the summer when he was a student.) *Now Eriskay, island of music* . . . *Iona of the saints* . . . Kisses, beautiful names, stars. We drift northwards all night under this hard creaking blanket. (But I chose him too.) I was a swan that morning. It was the final performance, an Arts Council recital in the Seamen's Institute, singing and flutes and dancing. Only a sprinkling of whalers in the front seats, belching beersmells and lewdness at us. Then the music guttered. Swans floated serene into The Black Flame. I was in river oil, alone, a fluttering clogged clamorous bird. Hard curves beat on me. I was tangled in oars. David lifted me out of that web. Now the sun labours up out of the mist, a gout of blood. And David turns from me again to the harder curve of the oar.

Teresa

Sanctus said the girls in the school choir. The nuns knelt like a flock of reverend penguins, beads looped in fingers. The Star of the Sea gave me a sweet plaster glance. *Benedictus qui venit in nomine Domini*, we said raggedly. Father Mulvaney bent down and kissed the altar. The Lord had entered Jerusalem on the ass. We strewed our bored offerings in the chapel air. *Hosanna in excelsis* I said. (I always picture the Mass like that — it is the life of Our Lord unfolding.) Gloria — that was the shepherds and angels in the stable. The Gospel was parables and miracles in Galilee; we were there at the roadside, watching, listening, wondering. Now *Hosanna* — the King was in the gate of the Holy City. After that glad shout, silence. The priest murmurs his prayers inaudibly. Soon men are going to commit their wickedest worst crime yet, the murder of God. The bread and wine are on the altar. In silence the Passion goes on — Gethsemane, the kiss, the scourging, the spittle, the mockery, the ring of thorns. Soon Christ must stumble up his fourteen stations to Golgotha. The bell rang in the sanctuary, like hammer on nail, a small sweet terrible music. Then nothing; this boat, the strange faces, bogs and beaches, the desolation going on and on. Father Mulvaney's Mass did not end. Between Sanctus and consecration The Black Flame came down: hosts and chalice lie among smouldering stones. (I remember nothing.) The desolation goes on and on and on. We never reached the empty tomb in the garden. Who is the saint of this sea now — I forget — is it Columbus? No, here it is, in the missal, Columba: 'he fished and ploughed and carved crosses on the stone' . . . Columba, pray for us. That flushed hulk we passed at sunset was Cape Wrath, Simon says. These black lumps on the sea against the dawn, he says, are the Orkneys. The missal again — here it is, Magnus: 'his skull was breached in a furrow on a day of new fires' . . . Magnus of Orkney, saint and virgin and martyr, have a care of the world's last few gutterings of breath.

Marilyn

'Appleblossom' they call me. Nice in a way, I suppose, but still I don't care a lot for it. The women give me my right name. The Skipper calls me nothing at all. Appleblossom — it makes me feel like one of them Japanese good-time girls. Well, I know my skin's pink-and-white. And if my eyes slant a bit it's quite attractive. And my small feet too. If it comes to that, I *do* feel like an applebranch simply bursting all over with flowers whenever Conrad or David look up from the oars. Time I had some romance, I'm fifteen. I don't think I fancy Simon very much. Siegfried the oarsman on the right side, he has a beautiful beard, simply a fleece of gold from his nostrils to his throat. The Skipper, he eyes every woman but me like a farmer in an auction ring, even the blind woman and that old bitch of a nurse that won't talk to a soul and her that's out with her holy Roman beads whenever a bigger wave than usual hits us. John the oarsman on the right side next the bow is just a boy — a science student, they say — he grows apples in his face whenever I so much as look at him. (I don't fancy him much either.) Disgraceful the way David and that dancer — stripper, most likely — carry on, trying to hide their goings-on under a sail (as if we can't hear them going at it half the night). Conrad, he has simply the nicest way of watching the stars, Natasha, the seabirds. I like Conrad. He used to write text-books on ecology, Natasha says, whatever that is. But this is really what I'd like to happen, The Skipper just to say to me quite simply, no nonsense (and when the time came I would shake all the apples on the tree down on him till I was stark as winter), *Marilyn, I want you for my woman.*

Trudi

What do you expect to find? I said to Saul the Skipper, (I wore his duffle in the stern last night, it was so cold.) *Better just settle,* I said, *for a foreshore with a spring of water in it,* I said, *and a cave or two under the crags. We must study the life of otters,* I said. *No Avalon or Hesperides or Tir-Nan-Og in this latitude.* He never said a word. He kept striking matches and looking at his chart in the darkness. I woke in the early morning. Crags rose sheer out of the sea, like pillars of fire. I don't think Saul had slept all night. He set his brow against every new headland as if he wanted to butt it down. Then about noon the crags dropped their swords, they turned from us, they knelt, fell, were red shoulders and knees sticking out of the water. I saw first a streak of sand, then a quiet tumult of brown and green fields. A burn flashed here and there, then ravelled itself among shore boulders, pink and blue and saffron spheroids, the heaped immaculate sculpture of the sea. The oarsmen and the

85

women (even Jane) turned their faces to this sweet green gap. Saul pushed the tiller away from him hard and the *Truelove* circled round under hosts of white wings rising and falling about the wake of our landfall.

HOUSES

Jane

I'm blind but there are one or two things I can do in this new
place. All morning I've been taking bits of wool from
thistles and barbed wire. The place is full of sheep
running half wild. Siegfried is my eyes. In some ruin or
other he found a wooden wheel and a frame and treadle.
That's for spinning, he said. *I'll find out the way myself
first and then I'll teach your fingers.* Finally The Skipper
showed us how it was done. So there may be a few
woollen shirts for next winter. And Siegfried's going to
take me to the hill when blackberries are out. I've
woven a rush basket for that. There'll be jam next
winter too, bitter I expect because there's no sugar. Will
we find a bees' nest in July? The place Siegfried is re-
building for us out of a ruin on the hillside, one wall is
finished. Siegfried took me to the gable this morning and
put my hands on the stones of the new wall and the sun
was warm on the stones. *The boy,* said Siegfried, *will
have the eyes that you lost in The Black Flame. I think
our children will grow up happy here, in Rackwick.*

Natasha

A host of cold voices greeted us in Rackwick — tern, skua,
plover, lark, kittiwake, heron, diver, dotterel. Only the
pigeons, though, come about the thresholds, looking for
the old peace offering between man and dove, a crumb
of bread. But till Conrad cuts our first harvest there's
no bread to offer. Still the birds of God at every door
insist on peace and friendship. One split the first tempest,
a branch-bearer, and fell through shivering rainbows on
the Ark. They tell us too, over and over — life can begin
again. A hard existence though until the first harvest is
cut in Rackwick. We eat boiled limpets and crabs till our
guts loathe them. The wild rams run from Conrad and
the other men into the hills. A northerly gale, a deluge
of rain, a hidden worm might blast the acres of sown
corn. But the dove goes from door to door among the
seven houses always. I take this for a good sign. (Why do

87

I love all these birds? I think they remind me of the lost music. My violin was shaped like some sweet archaic bird — yet it was very young as sounds go, three centuries perhaps — now it lies furled forever on the far side of The Black Flame, a delicate cinder. Lark and curlew, they cry on from beginning to end.) The Skipper says he will bring me a hawk from the hill.

Bianca

Venus every night, shaking out her yellow hair in the bay. Now it isn't as bad as it was in the boat, a rampage of lust. They have paired off decently with each other, six couples. They live in the six stone ruins and I'm alone, thank God, in a new wooden hut beside the marsh. Conrad and the musical woman, they have their house where the burn empties into the sea above the sand and the multi-coloured boulders. David and Sophie live under the little green hill that rises half-way between the horns of the bay. The Skipper's house is above the anchorage, looking south. Trudi is his woman, for the moment at least — his eyes flame everywhere like a goat before rutting time. The young silly ones, Marilyn and John, are higher up, towards Moorfea, near the kestrels. Siegfried with his bright beard does nothing but get gulls' eggs. His house is a ruckle, he has shifted a few stones, that's all. The blind woman will have many a hungry winter with the likes of him. Simon and Teresa, their house is at the glen where the burn drops down, loud and heather-hidden — and what would her priest and her nuns think of her now? Simon fishes with The Skipper. (But when all's said and done they're still rutting and rooting about in this place, no better than animals.) I live alone half-way between hills and sea — a small stretch of moss — in a hut of bleached boards. The Skipper gathered them for me, a few one day and a few another, whatever the sea threw up. Then off with him, like a billy-goat, among the crofts where the young women are.

Sophie

He turns from me, as soon as it's light, to the harder curve of the plough. After he had patched up the house he roofed the old stable and barn, to show his faith. Our green corn is tallest of all now. The Skipper isn't pleased about that. First David had to dig with a spade. Not a single ox had come through The Black Flame. There was one old plough rusting in the bog. And of course the tractor that belonged to the first inhabitants, it was worse than useless; even the rats and birds kept away from it; the petrol smell clings about it, faintly, like a ghost of the last age. Well, one day when David was among the hills didn't two horses cross the heather towards him, very delicate and shy, shaggy garrons, a mare with a black mane spilling into the wind and her foal. And at last the mare came right up to him and fitted her skull into his warm welcoming hand. And then David led her and the snickering foal home to the plough and empty stable. That plough leans against the wall brighter, I swear, than The Plough in the January sky. And here's something, there's another ripeness in the world. Deep inside me a new heaviness stirs and sways, poised, the sea-begotten dancer.

Teresa

Saint Magnus, or The Skipper, or just pure luck, brought us safe ashore. The *Truelove* ended against a rock, it's true. One by one we women dropped up to our throats in the bay and walked slowly ashore, bright shivering creatures. The men followed. The Skipper held the sack of seed corn high above his head. The seven houses are roofed now, some better than others. I wouldn't care to live in Jane's hovel, but she doesn't know, she's blind, and so pleased with her Siegfried everything he does is perfect. Simon, he's learning to be a fisherman. I prayed my rosary thin all the shortening nights of spring, asking for some kind of a blessing on our bed. We must live now as if we existed in some poor pagan ballad, unparadised, Simon and I. The sun rose and set but Good Friday went

89

on and on, the last breath guttering in the throat of God.
There must have been a few women who spat and
laughed and gossiped under the Cross — surely I belonged
with them And another woman stood among us, cold
with grief, turned away from me, hidden. Better a
thousand times to have ended in grace in The Black
Flame. It was more than I could bear. Six nights ago I
put my faith from me, I threw my rosary in the midden.
I stood in the door then, purified. I drew breath within
a crude ballad, with only a few rhymes (grave-wave-
weave: thorn-mourn-corn.) Not again would the scatter
of notes that was me, my identity, my selfhood, Teresa,
be caught up in the transfiguring music of any Mass or
Benediction. It was best that way. This morning I went
down to the wooden house at the moss — Bianca con-
firmed what I had known for weeks — I was pregnant.
I left her and her cold smiles. I climbed the hill to our
house. What would I do? I would stand in the open door.
I would say to Simon, *We are both hungry. There will
soon be a new hunger in this house, a child, a bastard.*
I stood in the door. Simon was making a creel. I could
say nothing. Simon looked up. I went out again. I stood
between house and byre. Simon followed me. He said,
This is good news, Teresa. Siegfried hailed me joyfully
across the valley. David cried from the burn, *Well done,
Teresa.* The ballad (earth-dearth-birth) dissolved in a
Gloria of fisherman and shepherd and ploughman. I
stooped down in the midden. I wiped the fish-slime and
dung from the bone beads. My rosary, for the Third
Joyful Mystery, slipped through my fingers like corn
seed, like drops of sweet water.

Marilyn

I want you for my woman, The Skipper said to me. He was
up at Moorfea helping John to put mortar on the wall.
No, I said, *I have a man, and your woman is Trudi.* John
was away at the burn getting water to mix the cement.
The Skipper just laughed. *You will come when I'm
ready,* he said. Then when the houses were roofed and
the fields sown we all went down to the moor to cut

peat. *Be careful of that Billy-goat,* old Bianca said to me. The Skipper sank his spade in next to mine. He said, *You will come and live at my place the day after tomorrow . . . My house is at Moorfea,* I said, *John and I live there. John is my man. I love him.* We stayed behind to spread out the wet peats when the others went home — The Skipper, Bianca, and me. The first stars came out. Bianca shouldered her spade and went home, smiling. *I will look after you better than that fool of a boy,* said The Skipper in the darkness. He unbuttoned my shirt and probed my breasts with his hand the way a farmer will examine the first apples. Then the thing was done. *Trudi knows about this,* he said. *You will come to my place before harvest. Soon everybody here will work for me. This is the way it must be. That boy will be given his place.*

Trudi

A host of gulls, rising and falling and screaming about his basket of fish. He's dragging the boat up, he and Simon. No peace in the man at all. He was out before first light making a fence. Now he'll eat, then sleep an hour. Then up to the hill with him to speak to the hawk. Yesterday it came down and sat on his wrist a minute, then flew into the cloud again. (He has promised the hawk to Natasha.) He took the wild ram by the horns last week — it's tethered at the end of the house. There's that bull near the Kame, he says, and a stallion somewhere in the Trowieglen. He hewed querns from an immense boulder at the beach, stone circles out of a stone sphere. He has put new strakes in the *Truelove* — they'll fish miles out in the Pentland next spring. Even our bowels is his concern. *Dung and bread are brothers,* he tells them. *Don't unbreech in the heather, save it for the furrows . . .* Then he must settle the dispute between Bianca and David of Greenhill, some patch of heather where she wants to spread her washing. He digs drains everywhere. He broods over every fish, every cornshoot, with his great eyes, to see if The Black Flame has worked some mutation. He says he made a big mistake at landfall: they should have built one large house, a Hall, not squandered their strength on the seven hovels. *I'll put all that to rights,* he says, and when The Skipper and I should be sleeping we heave up stones from the beach to make this the one dominant house in the valley. There's no rest in the man. I don't like him. But he brought us safe out of The Black Flame. He saved the seed corn. He taught the men how to fish and handle sheep. One thing I've found out, it's best to do exactly what he says; at least till our first harvest is cut.

HARVEST

Jane

The baby, Siegfried tells me, has two blue eyes. His mouth
is red like all mouths. Small and round and red and
cold, it tugs at my warm enriched breasts. He cries
often, more like the wail of a seabird than a butterfed
baby. The women go and come silently. The men are a
spectrum of voices among the ripening fields. Siegfried's
sowing was not a success. *I will take over your ploughing
next year,* said The Skipper. *Look at David's field, that's
the way corn should be at this time of year. Can I
trust you with sheep? I doubt it. Still you will have to
be our shepherd here in Rackwick.* So Siegfried looks
after the badtempered ram and the forty mild sheep that
were rounded up in the Trowieglen. The spinning wheel
goes for a while, then stops, then The Skipper comes to
hammer in a nail or re-set the treadle. Next winter will
there be coats for everybody in the valley? The child
with the ploughman's legs and fisherman's arms will have
the first gray coat. All the women, says Siegfried, are in
different stages of pregnancy. The women are a spectrum
of ripeness across the valley. The Rackwick children
will be five or six years old about the same time. Maybe
then they'll want me for a teacher again: but no history,
and no poetry, and only enough mathematics for them
to count to a hundred. Beyond that, the black circle of
Mephistopheles. We broke into it. We were burned.

Natasha

I have the hawk. The day before harvest The Skipper came
down from The Ward with a struggling sack. At the door
of Burnmouth he opened the sack and set the bird on
my wrist. Conrad was at the edge of the field, honing a
scythe. The Skipper crossed over to Conrad. They
greeted each other; their bodies inclined for a minute,
a murmuring arch; then their heads swung apart and
they mingled voices, one sweet terrible cry. Conrad
flashed at The Skipper with his scythe and cut a ribbon
of skin from his arm. I could do nothing, the hawk sat

on my hand and encompassed me in a wide yellow glare. The Skipper struck Conrad with his fist and Conrad fell among the corn. The Skipper came back and took the hawk from me. The hawk's claw had pierced a vein in my wrist. The Skipper mixed some of the blood from his arm with the blood scattering off my knuckles like heavy red coins. I followed him across three fields to the Shore. Bianca, old mute mockery, stood in her door. Trudi kissed me in the threshold. Marilyn arched like a cat against the wall. There was a new cold room ready for me. Next day I helped in The Skipper's barley harvest. At the other side of the bay Conrad works alone in his field. The hawk sits in the dark of the barn. The pigeons have shifted from this door to Conrad's door and to David and Sophie's door and to the blank bolted door of Moorfea.

Bianca

I didn't think King Goat would break his tether and rut and rampage as far as that! First that trash of a girl Marilyn in the peatbog, and now Natasha. They live, if you please, at The Shore now, and not a cry out of Trudi or out of John (the boy is simple-minded, he has the guts of a sparrow.) Conrad works on by himself in his field. We will see what we will see. The blind woman, she'll be next, I knew it. The Skipper has made her man the shepherd, if you please, Siegfried. Saul is the master here, he has one aim, to fill the valley with a torrent of his own goats. To him the women are nothing but walking wombs, seed jars. The children to come will all wear his face — the fishermen, shepherds, crofters, tinkers, blacksmiths, millers, beachcombers, fiddlers. The other men are too gentle, or too stupid, or too weak, to breed the only kind of animal that can survive in this place. I know for sure now why I have sufferance here, so that whole and sound the new tribe can be brought from womb to cradle. So he comes with his animal eyes and cold charity of fish to me, a cold sybil.

94

Sophie

Sea-begotten, earth-born. I laid the baby in a corner of the
    field. Our barley was green yesterday. Overnight it
    changed colour, as if the sun was looking into a huge
    wind-flawed mirror. *Time for scythes,* said David. How
    can a dancer become a harvester in one day? My first
    cuttings were brief and mangled. I learned quickly from
    David. By noon the swathes of corn fell before me, cut
    clean to the bottom of the stalk. We did the Dance of
    Bread together, David and I. Once The Skipper came to
    the edge of our barley. He shouted at us but we paid no
    attention. I think he wanted us to work in his corn
    first — his field is a host of labourers and a scattering of
    thin stooks. Late in the afternoon I went over to the
    corner of the field and opened my blouse and fed the
    baby. David trudged on, the scythe flashing round his
    loins like strokes of lightning, till the last of the barley
    was cut. Then I brought water from the burn to the
    mare and her foal. Larksong above the red fires west-
    ward, a rapture of quick small hidden dancers. David
    carried the scythes into the barn and laid them bright
    beside the smouldering plough. I went to pick up the
    baby from the corner of the field. He wasn't there! I
    took my arms out of the cold burn. I stumbled a few
    steps towards the eagle's nest on the hill. The Skipper
    stood in the marsh with a bundle in his arms. I screamed
    at him but my legs sank in to the knees. David stood up
    to his thighs in the quaking earth. He held out his hands.
    The Skipper laughed. Then he walked surefooted through
    the marsh like a man on a hard road. He laid the baby
    beside the whetstone. *Some day,* he said, *this man will
    come of his own free will. And so will you, David and
    Sophie. I need your plough and horses.*

Teresa

Corn-seed, drops of sweet water. 'Eat thy bread with joy and
    drink thy wine with a merry heart.' Yes, but nothing is
    said about the brutal stations from winter to the loaf
    and jar that are not yet on the table — plough, furrow,

seed, harrows, the scarecrow, scythe, flail, fan, millstones, the vat and the oven. We stand between scythe
and flail, bewildered. I know I can never adore again
when the Host is raised. But I think there is a kind of
holiness in coarse mortal bread too, men labour and
sweat so hard to set it on their tables. Next month
there'll be a new hunger, a child in the cradle, longed-
for, loved, unhallowed. Yesterday they caught no fish
at all. Simon came home with a long blue stone from
the ebb. *I'm not going to break this one up for creel-
weights,* he said. *It's for you, you like beautiful shapes.*
I could have yelled at him, I was so hungry. Then I
looked at the stone and the God-Bearer moved in it.
(The last thing that had filled my eyes was Our Lady
Star of the Sea in the school chapel.) Had she come to us
through The Black Flame? I looked again. It was only a
stone. The wayward hands of the sea had sculpted a
purity. Yet there are faint chisellings that might be eyes.
Did an old mason, a hewer of querns and tombstones,
carve it for their first chapel? The Rackwick folk, did
they hide it under seaweed from the horsemen of Knox?
I'm sorry about the fish, said Simon. I looked again.
The women of Rackwick moved through the stone,
the sea-watchers, generations of them: the girls, the
young wives, the mothers, widows, the very old ones,
An endless surge of grief and patience had gone into the
stone. *It is only a stone,* said Simon. It was indeed only
a stone that the sea had washed, a tall immaculate blue
stone. *Leave it alone,* said Simon. *I want my supper.
There's enough limpets for a boiling. We put creels
under Rora. I must be up and out early.* I set the fold
of stone against the wall. I think of Our Lady, and the
child, and I pray that he will be born near that stone in
the heart of winter.

Marilyn

John was well and truly put in his place last night — plenty
of outcry at the end of the house. John had broken the
blade of the second scythe in the barley field, in the
afternoon. *The stone was hidden,* he said, *I couldn't*

help it. The Skipper sent him back to the house. *Go in,* he said, *you are not an earth-worker. Slowly we find our vocations. This is what you truly are, a beachcomber. Beachcombing is a mystery. There will be an initiation.* At sunset The Skipper called to Natasha and Trudi and me to come out. We left the haddocks simmering over the fire. John hung shivering like a hooked fish at the gable end; his wrists thonged to the iron bolt under the chimney head. *This man will never be a crofter, or a fisherman, or a shepherd,* said The Skipper. *I am going to initiate him into the ancient mystery of beachcombing. I am going to change him into a gull, a scavenger. Trudi,* he said, *the whip.* Trudi, cold-faced, came out of the barn with the coiled leather snake. Natasha turned her face towards the hills. *Now, gull,* said The Skipper, *go into this man.* The lash sang. The face against the stone crumpled and gasped. Lash sang, mouth gaped and gasped. Lash sang and sang, forty-eight times, but still the changing body did not admit its new state by one single cry. I had not known my John to have so much courage. From their doors the valley people watched. The Skipper stopped at last, his chest heaving. *Cut the boy down,* said Natasha, her face still towards Moorfea, *Trudi and I will see to him . . . No,* said The Skipper, *no-one will touch him, he will stay where he is. The gull has not yet gone into him. Not yet. He must learn to be a beachcomber. This is what a beachcomber must often do, he must stand all night watching a flow and ebb. He must be patient as a bird till the sun gets up. It is not an easy thing, to be a beachcomber.* He went into the house. Natasha and Trudi and I stood about the flayed man. The sun went down. We did not speak. One by one we went to our separate beds. The Skipper came from Natasha's bed to my bed in the darkness, and parted my knees, and left again before sunrise. I stood in the door and watched him. He went naked into the sea. He swam far out and came back with a lobster, and threw it, high and thinly clashing, on the grass bank. Then he climbed up to the house and went cold and wet into

97

Trudi's bed. This is the kind of man he is. I went out to where our first beachcomber, still clothed in the tortured flesh of man, sagged at the wall. I whispered to the skewered head. *We will eat and drink next winter.* The body was silent. During the night, though stationary, it had travelled back a great distance. *Someone must suffer,* I said, *I couldn't help what I did. You stood between me and the sun.* With the nail of my forefinger I loosened slowly a thick dark medal that soldered his rag of shirt to his shoulders; then tore it off. A circle of new blood oozed and darkened and welled. I broke the red disc between my fingers. The sunken head rose up like a bird. The scavenger turned cold eyes on me. He shrieked, a gull in the first light.

Trudi

We have done everything exactly as he said. Now it is Harvest Home at The Hall (what was once called Shore). On the table that I have scrubbed to its pale yellow graining lie pieces of fish and ribs of mutton. Their mouths glister with salt. No-one speaks. Flame drips and drips from the fish-oil lamp: the four walls are splashed with a carnival of shadows. Their mouths are silent as a shoal of fish mouths. Quiet glimmering people, they eat meagrely in the centre of a wild flaring shadow-festival. They are imprisoned in their own night and winter and death.

It is Harvest Home (even though the crop has failed.) The corn died, and from now on Saul's people will be fishermen, and women who watch the sea. The sheaves were safely stacked under the equinox. They leaned like dancers holding each other up, three by three against the splash of sunset, tired after their light summer dancings. The morning after the equinox we all rose early to hump the sheaves into the barn. I stood first in the door — the field was pitted with rottenness — where the sheaves had stood were smears and daubings of gray treacle. *The Black Flame scorched the seed,* said Saul. *We were not to know. No-one will mention the word corn again in this valley. We will turn to the sea* . . . Jane's baby died. She lifted him up one morning to feed him; the small mouth was open and stiff as a haddock's . . . *Sometimes there are whales,* said Saul. *They come into this bay, a school of whales. Every whale is a storehouse of meat and oil.* Nobody answered him. There is little talk any more. They nod here and there with their foreheads, their hands make shapes in the smoke. The fish-oil light wrenches each simple gesture into a silent threat and portent on one or other of the four walls.

It is Harvest Home; now the reason will appear. One small sack of barley was saved, enough to make one jar of ale. With bitter care Natasha and I brooded over the malting, the steeping, the boiling, the fermentation. Now it is ready, a thin swill in a clay pot. Saul nods to John the beachcomber. John rises. He takes the jar from the cupboard. The ale glows in the vessel like a lamp that has lit the feet of men from Babylon to Hiroshima, a merry wayfaring, a sacred storied centuries-long procession. Now the pilgrimage is nearly over. The sweet oil of Barleycorn is all but spent. John brings the ceremonial jar to Saul. He kneels, he delivers it. Saul drinks: patriarch, law-giver, priest, keeper of seed, measurer of the west, laird. The acolyte takes the cup from him. He brings the cup to Siegfried. (We age quickly in this place, Siegfried's golden beard is a badger's pelt hung from his jaws.) Bianca looks very solemn. Siegfried drinks, inclining his face towards Saul. *With the sun,* Natasha cries out, her mouth a savage harp. Simon raises his sea-carbuncled hands to take the cup from Siegfried. Bianca smiles. Teresa makes a cross over the chalice as it passes her face, sunwards, going to Simon. Simon raises the cup. He nods briefly to Saul. Jane stares blankly at the blank wall. Simon drinks. Natasha is silent. Bianca's mouth quivers. Simon sets down the empty jar on the table. The corn lamp is out. John lifts the jar and returns it to The Skipper. The Skipper folds it in his hands. He stands up. He holds the cup over us. He says,

Flung we a broad far sail,
Sought, beyond whale and star wheel
A maiden meadow. Blossomed the mew,
Salt beads on prow scattered,
Was league on league of lost landfall,
Flame of the atom behind us,
In front, green flames of ice.
In cragfolds found we haven,
After hard voyage a hidden valley,
Hills for bees to be hived,
Beasts kept, a cod-hungry boat,
A comfort of fire in the crofts.
We furled sail, set firm our feet,
Stone laid against stone,
Laboured long till ebb of light,
Hungry men round a half-made hearth.
Dreamed I that darkness
Of horse, harp, a hallowed harvest.

The Skipper opens his hands over us in a kind of benediction. The pot falls on the floor and breaks, a small crash and scatter. Bianca wails, she alone, a cry like a woman in hard travail. The fish people sit round the table. The lamp drips and glims and smokes. We sit quiet in the midst of an enormous jerking masquerade. In silence and frenzy the shadows feast on us. They hollow out our skulls. We have returned, uncaring, into the keeping of the Dragon.